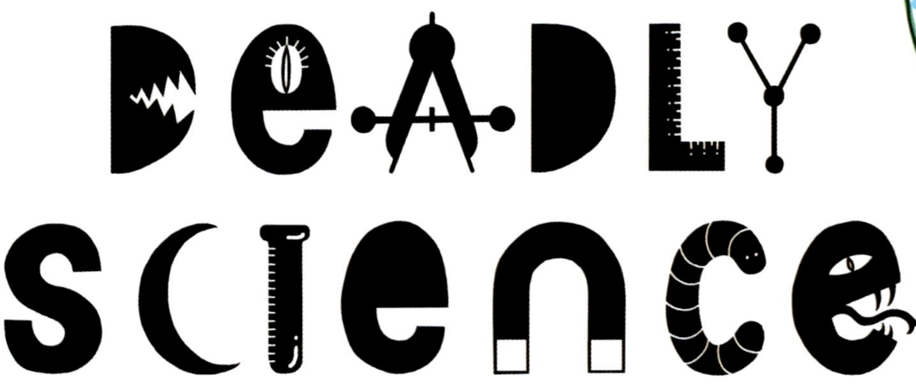


## Earth's changing surfaces

**Contents:**

ADJUNCT ASSOCIATE PROFESSOR COREY TUTT OAM

### DEADLYSCIENCE

DeadlyScience aims to provide Science, Technology, Engineering and Mathematics (STEM) resources to remote schools around Australia. So far, DeadlyScience has shipped more than shipped more than 33,000 STEM books and resources to more than 800 schools across the country.

The organisation began when proud Kamilaroi man Corey Tutt found out that some schools in Australia were completely under-resourced and that Aboriginal and Torres Strait Islander children were discouraged from pursuing STEM because of this. DeadlyScience knows from personal experience that books and resources change lives and believes these kids deserve nothing but the best. Aboriginal and Torres Strait Islander peoples in Australia were the First Scientists of this land, and DeadlyScience is committed to preserving that history.

# Inside Earth

Our planet is not simply a ball of rock. The inner core is solid, very hot and made up of iron and nickel. The outer core is liquid but also comprised of iron and nickel. Next, the mantle can be divided into two sections. The bottom section is the asthenosphere, which is made of slowly flowing rock. Above that is a more rigid section that, together with the Earth's crust, makes up a layer called the lithosphere. The crust is made of vast, rocky slabs called tectonic plates. There are seven particularly large plates that correspond with the seven continents. The plates float on top of the molten rock of the asthenosphere, moving constantly. When the plates hit each other, they can cause earthquakes, or they can push upward to form mountains. If magma from the mantle comes up through these mountains, they can erupt as volcanoes.

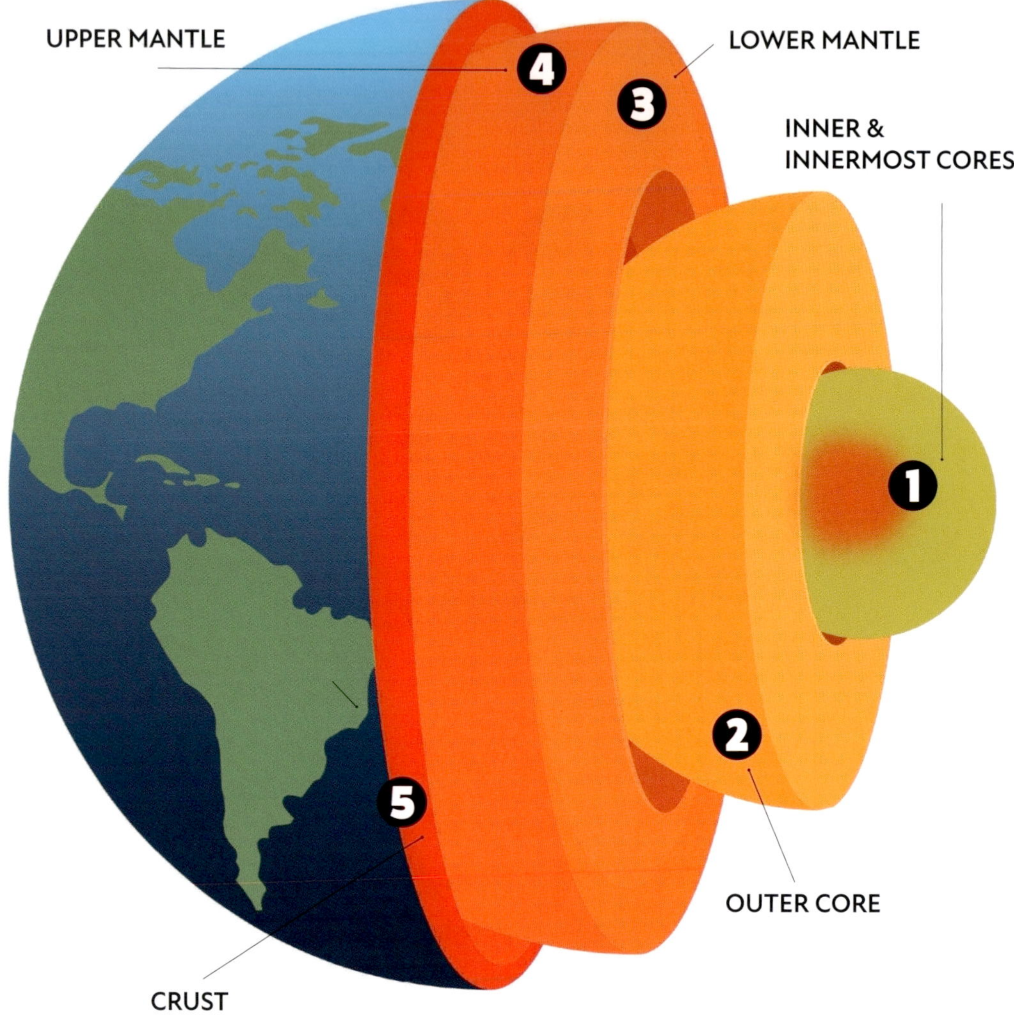


## THE STRUCTURE OF THE EARTH

The solid rocks of Earth's crust shift and move on top of the hot rocks and magma of the mantle. The energy comes from an inner core that's as hot as the surface of the Sun.

**1 Inner and innermost cores**
The innermost core is the hottest layer and was recently discovered. Amazingly, the inner and innermost cores don't melt, due to pressure from above.

**2 Outer core**
Iron and nickel have melted into a 2200 km thick outer core.

**3 Lower mantle**
This is also known as the mesosphere, and this is where hot rock (4000 °C) is under enormous pressure.

**4 Upper mantle**
This largely solid rock is up to 640 km thick and extends from just below the Earth's crust. The two parts of the upper mantle are the lithosphere and the asthenosphere.

**5 Crust**
The Earth's crust is very thin – it's 5 km thick under the sea and 70 km thick beneath continents.

## The Himalayas

These mighty mountains between the Indian Subcontinent and the Tibetan Plateau formed slowly when huge tectonic plates collided.

1. About 200 million years ago, the landmass that is now India began to move northward towards Asia.
2. India and Asia collided, and the crust was pushed upward to form mountains.
3. Today, more than 50 million years later, the Himalayas are still being pushed higher.

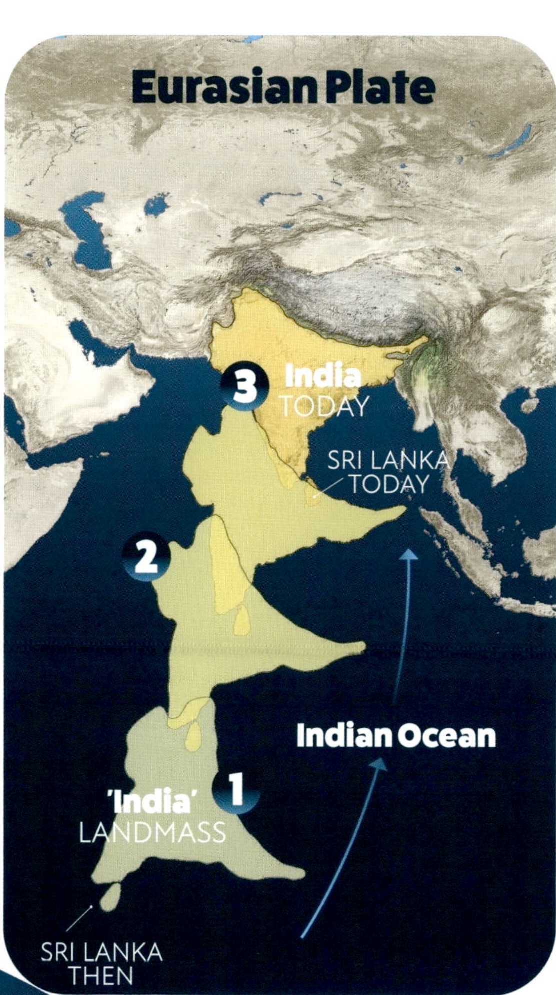

**FACT**
When continental plates collide, they can create huge mountains, like 8849-m-tall Mt Everest, the world's tallest peak.

## Fault lines

Just like bones, rocks can fracture under extreme pressure. These fractures, or fault lines, appear in the Earth's crust where two or more tectonic plates meet. When rocks on each side of the fault line grind against each other, an earthquake can occur. Some of the well-known faults include the Himalayan Fault, which gave rise to the world's highest mountain range; the San Andreas Fault, in the United States; New Zealand's Southern Alps; and the Ring of Fire in the Pacific Ocean.

## Collision course

Tectonic plates can collide with great force. When this happens, mountains, volcanoes, earthquakes, and deep ocean trenches are created.

## Mountain makers

Tectonic plates beneath huge landmasses are called continental plates. When these collide, the mountains they create are very high. The Eurasian and Indian plates produced the Himalayas – the world's tallest mountains.

## PLATE TECTONICS THEORY

MOUNTAIN RANGE
HIGH PLATEAU
CONTINENTAL CRUST
CONTINENTAL CRUST
LITHOSPHERE
LITHOSPHERE
ASTHENOSPHERE

# Supercontinents

Millions of years ago, all of the land on Earth was joined as one enormous supercontinent known as Pangaea. Then, 200 million years ago, this giant body of land began to break apart, creating smaller supercontinents named Gondwana and Laurasia. These two eventually broke apart as well, and the continents drifted, finally forming the world as we know it today.

## Gondwana

Gondwana, when it formed, contained the land that made up most of the countries that are now part of the Southern Hemisphere – including Antarctica, South America, Africa and Australia, as well as India and the Arabian Peninsula (although these have since moved north). It began to break up about 184 million years ago, as Antarctica, Madagascar, India and Australia began to separate from Africa. Australia, one of the youngest continents, only separated from Antarctica about 80 million years ago.

## Laurasia

Laurasia was the supercontinent that formed in the north. It was mostly made up of the countries that now form part of the Northern Hemisphere, including the United States and most of Asia. North America and the west coast of Africa broke apart approximately 180 million years ago, and in the process, they created a brand-new ocean – the Atlantic Ocean. When Laurasia split, it divided into North America and Eurasia, which was the combined continents of Europe and Asia.

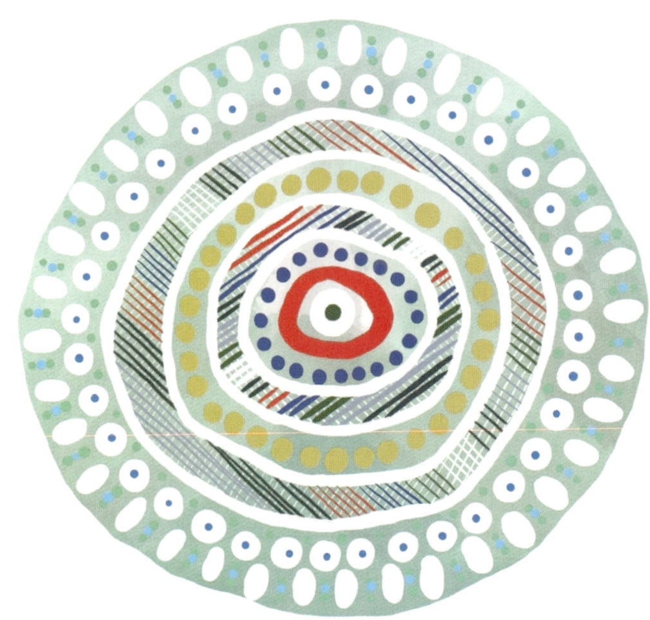

**Pangaea**
350 MILLION YEARS AGO

**Laurasia and Gondwana**
200 MILLION YEARS AGO

## Present day

**DID YOU KNOW?**

**DNA evidence shows that Aboriginal culture is the oldest in the world – it is at least 65,000 years old!**

## Proof

One of the pieces of evidence for this theory of supercontinents is the distribution of fossils. For example, fossils of the glossopteris ferns can be found in bands across South America, Africa, India and Australia – all from around 270 million years ago.

When botanist Sir Joseph Banks sailed around the world on the HMS *Endeavour* with Captain James Cook from 1768–71, he discovered trees that would provide some of the first clues to the processes of plate tectonics and continental drift.

One of those trees was Australia's only native, cold-climate, deciduous tree (which means it annually drops all its leaves) – the deciduous beech. It grows in remote highland regions of Tasmania, requiring cold winters and more than 1800 mm of rain annually to thrive and survive.

# Changing rocks

Rocks are pushed up by tectonic forces and then eroded by wind and rain. When molten rock cools, igneous rocks are formed. The debris from eroded rocks collects as layers of sediment. Over time, these layers are pressed together to form sedimentary rocks. Intense heat and pressure can transform these layers into metamorphic rocks.

## Incredible fossils

Sometimes, when an animal or plant dies, its remains are buried before they can decay. If conditions are right, the remains get preserved as fossils. Fossils are the ancient remains or traces of animals, plants and other organisms that have been preserved in the Earth's crust. Fossils may take the form of a shell, bone, tooth, leaf, or even footprint. Fossils can range in age from 3.5 billion-year-old traces of microscopic algae to 10,000-year-old remains of animals preserved during the last Ice Age.

**DID YOU KNOW?**

**Metamorphic rocks are formed by underground heat and pressure.**

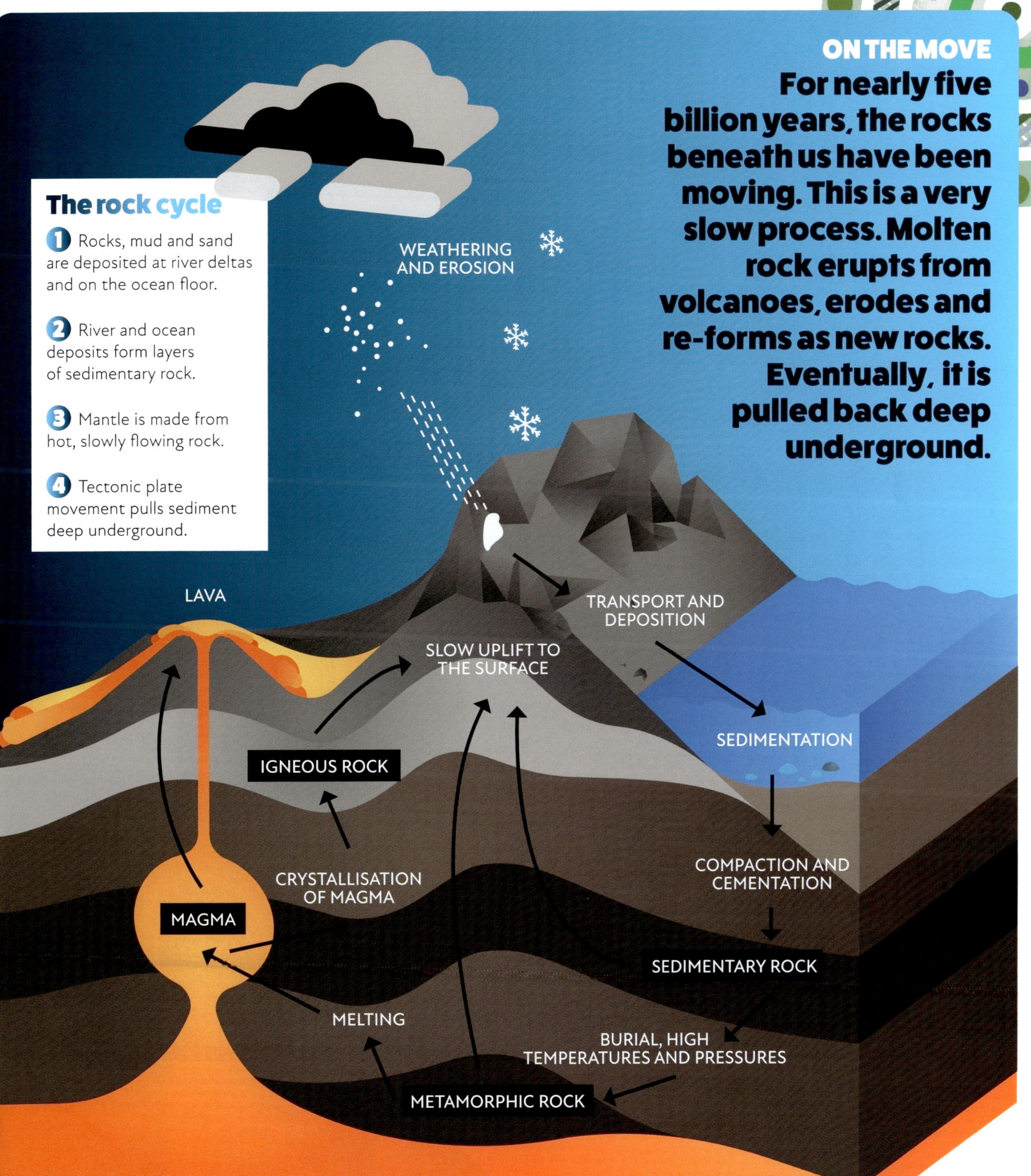


## The rock cycle

1. Rocks, mud and sand are deposited at river deltas and on the ocean floor.
2. River and ocean deposits form layers of sedimentary rock.
3. Mantle is made from hot, slowly flowing rock.
4. Tectonic plate movement pulls sediment deep underground.

## ON THE MOVE

**For nearly five billion years, the rocks beneath us have been moving. This is a very slow process. Molten rock erupts from volcanoes, erodes and re-forms as new rocks. Eventually, it is pulled back deep underground.**

TOTEM POLE, TAS

# Igneous rocks

Igneous rocks are formed when molten rock cools and solidifies. Rocks that form deep within the Earth's crust at very high temperatures can take thousands of years to cool down. This makes the crystals much larger, such as in the case of granite. In contrast, igneous rocks formed on the surface cool down in a matter of hours. The crystals in these rocks can be microscopically small, and the rocks can look more shiny and glassy.

FINGAL HEAD CAUSEWAY, NSW

## Column formation

Rock columns are the result of ancient remains of old volcanic cones and their lava flows. As the softer surrounding rock is gradually eroded, large cathedral-like columns begin to emerge.

### 1 Cooling lava

The lava shrinks as heat is lost to the air from its surface and to the ground from underneath.

### 2 Tension cracks

Tiny cracks appear as tension increases over the surface. The cracks begin to grow towards the hot centre.

### 3 Complete columns

Columns form as the cracks from the top and bottom of the lava flow join up with each other in the centre.

## Amazing structures

The vertical columns at Fingal Head, NSW, look like they've been chiselled out of rock, but they were formed when volcanic basalt erupted. As the lava cooled, incredible hexagonal columns emerged. The same geological phenomenon occurred in Northern Ireland and created the famous Giant's Causeway.

## Basalt sands

Black Beach, at Kiama on the NSW coast, gets its name from the igneous basaltic sand and cobbles that line its shores.

KIAMA, NSW

NATURAL BRIDGE, SPRINGBROOK NP, QLD

## Australian volcanic formations

While there are no active volcanoes on the Australian mainland, some landscapes were formed by earlier volcanic activity. The eruption of the Tweed Volcano formed the mountains of Springbrook and Lamington National Parks. Huge columns of dolerite line the cliffs at the southern end of Tasmania. Formed by cooling magma, these hexagonal columns rise hundreds of metres out of the sea. In far north Queensland some 190,000 years ago, Undara volcano erupted with a long gush of lava. It filled valleys, and although the surface cooled into a hard crust, lava surged below. More than 160 km of lava tubes, tunnels and arches were created.

**FACT**

Crushed ochre, or iron oxide, and yellow clay are used in traditional ceremonies.

# Sedimentary rocks

Over millions of years, igneous rocks are weathered by forces of wind and water until they transform into small rock particles that are carried to the bottom of lakes and oceans. Slowly, the layer of sediment grows deeper and deeper, reaching depths of thousands of metres. The immense weight of all the sediment pushes with tremendous downward force onto lower layers. This process, combined with minerals that act like cement or glue, bond the sediment together to form sedimentary rock.

**DID YOU KNOW?**

**The ochre paints used in ancient Aboriginal rock art across the country have stood the test of time. At Murujuga in Western Australia, the rock art is at least 40,000 to 60,000 years old.**

## Patience makes perfect

Canyons are formed when water flows over a piece of land for millions of years. The water begins to cut deep into the rocks, carving out canyons and gorges along the way.

1. **PATHWAYS** form as sea levels fall or the land rises, and sedimentary rocks are exposed. Rivers and streams begin to cut narrow pathways through the land.
2. **LAND ERODES** as water cuts deeper into hard rock. When rivers reach softer layers, water digs underneath the harder rock.
3. **THE WATER** flowing underneath the hard rock causes the upper layers to collapse. Large mesas (flat-topped mountains) and valleys are widened.

## The Grand Canyon

A famous example of a large canyon formation is the Grand Canyon in Arizona, USA. This colossal canyon is made up of a thick stack of sedimentary layers that started forming almost two billion years ago.

**250 KAIBAB LIMESTONE**
The youngest layer is made up of tiny seashell fossils.

**255 TOROWEAP SANDSTONE**
Formed from sand deposited as the sea rose over the Coconino desert.

**260 COCONINO SANDSTONE**
Formed from desert sands when the sea was at its lowest.

**265 HERMIT SHALE**
Formed when rivers carried silt and mud onto a delta floodplain.

**285 SUPAI GROUP**
Formed when sea shallows and rivers brought mud and sand on top of earlier limestone.

**335 REDWALL LIMESTONE**
Formed as the shells of tiny creatures that died on the sea floor slowly built up over time.

**350 TEMPLE BUTTE LIMESTONE**
When the sea was at its highest level, life flourished in the warmer water.

**515 MUAV LIMESTONE**
When the sea completely flooded the land, tiny sea shells were deposited.

**530 BRIGHT ANGEL SHALE**
Formed from fine grains of silt and mud when the sea level rose over the Tapeats beaches.

**545 TAPEATS SANDSTONE**
The remains of a sandy beach that formed as the sea rose over the eroded Vishnu landscape.

**1800 VISHNU SCHIST**
The oldest rock layer was formed when mountain ranges were pushed up after two continents collided 1.8 billion years ago.

**FACT**
America's Grand Canyon is some 4930km$^2$, ranking it among the largest canyons in the world.

# Metamorphic rocks

These rocks form below the Earth's surface when heat and pressure are applied to either igneous rocks or sedimentary rocks. This heat and pressure 'cook' the rocks and greatly change their structure. The rocks partially melt, which transforms their chemical composition so that the final rock is very different to the original rock. A common metamorphic rock is marble, which forms when heat and pressure are applied to limestone over thousands of years. Another common one is slate, which forms out of shale and mudstone.

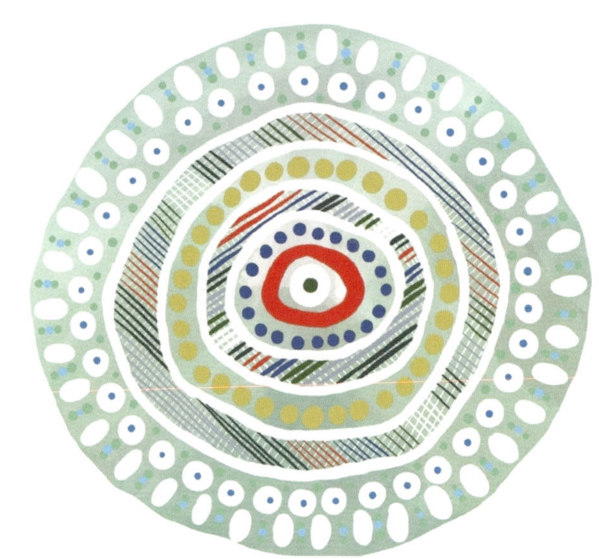

## 1 Regional metamorphism

This process begins when opposing forces on the tectonic plates begin to squeeze a large area of land. The opposing forces fold and crush the rocks, creating various kinds of metamorphic rocks, depending on the level of heat and pressure.

## 2 Contact metamorphism

This occurs when magma rises up through rock layers. The magma heats the surrounding stone and various metamorphic rocks are created, depending on the types of rocks present.

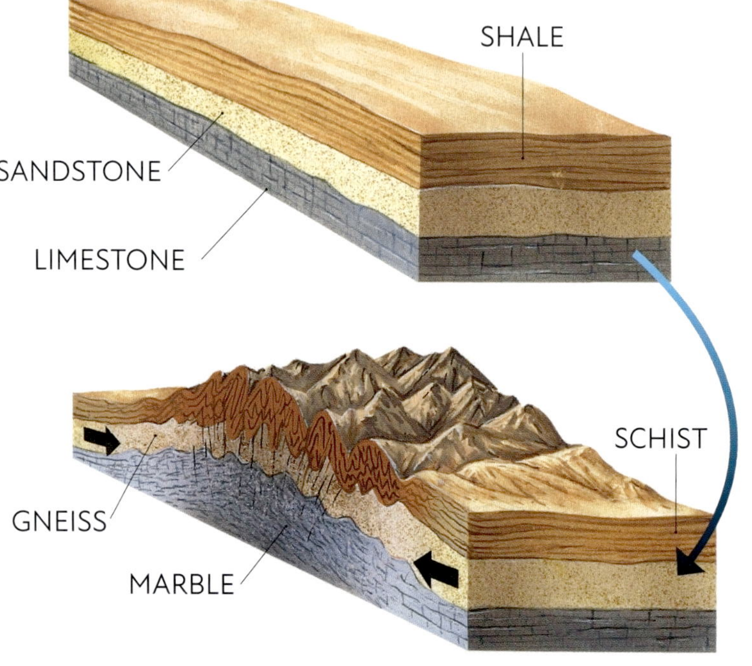


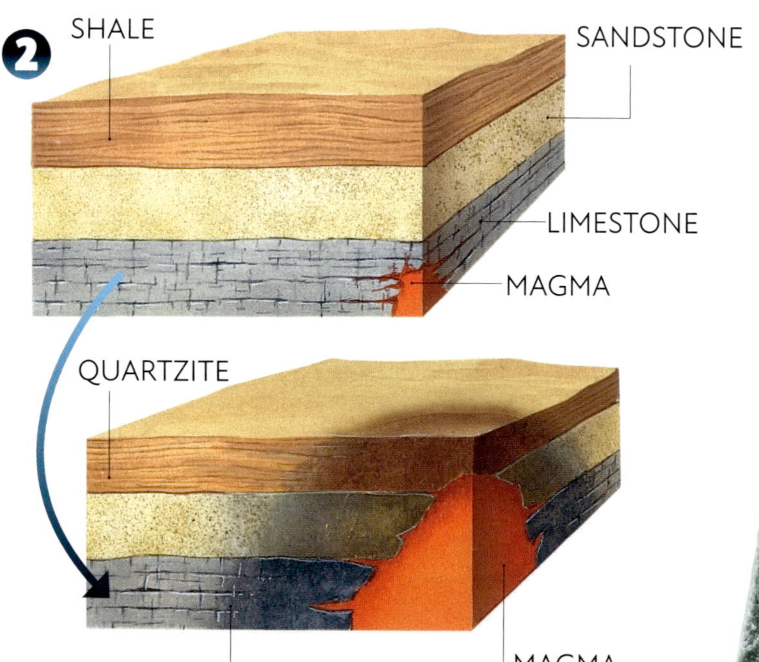

DID YOU KNOW?

**First Nations peoples carried pieces of sandstone with them so that they could sharpen their tools on the go.**

## Pressure yields results

Different types of metamorphic rocks form, depending on the pressure and heat applied to the rocks.

### 1 Phyllite

This type of layered metamorphic rock is primarily composed of quartz, sericite, mica and chlorite.

### 2 Amphibolite

Consisting mainly of hornblende amphibole, this is a dark-coloured, heavy rock.

### 3 Gneiss

This medium- or coarse-grained metamorphic rock is common and widely distributed.

### 4 Schist

This coarse-grained metamorphic rock often has a shiny appearance, as large mica crystals.

FACT

Australia's First Nations people made ground-edge axes by striking off large pieces of stone from rocky surfaces, and then grinding them into shape.

# Australia's amazing rocks

Uluṟu and Kata Tjuṯa, in the Northern Territory, were both created at the same time over 500 million years ago. They are the remains of a mountain range that had very little vegetation to protect it from winds and rain that broke it down, carrying the soil and rock away. These mountain ranges eventually almost completely eroded away, and Uluṟu and Kata Tjuṯa are all that remain. They were tightly folded when the mountains crinkled up, which may be why their rock is so hard, resistant, and uniform in colour.

KATA TJUṮA, NT

**FACT**
These rocks' red colour comes from their iron content. When iron is exposed to air and water, it changes from grey in colour to red.

## Devils Marbles

These incredible boulders, also called Karlu Karlu (which means round boulders), are located in the Northern Territory. They have great significance to the Traditional Owners of the land they are on – the Warumungu, Kaytete, Alyawarra and Warlpiri people. They were created when molten rock surged up and then cooled under sandstone. Water, time, and cracks broke down its surface, revealing the boulders.

## Bottoms up

The rocks of the Bungle Bungles formed in a similar way to Uluṟu. They have banded stripes of colour because this area used to sit at the bottom of a riverbed. Over the years, layers of different sediment settled on the bottom of a river. These layers compressed into sandstone and lifted up to form a mountain range.

## Names matter

The area around Uluṟu was first settled about 10,000 years ago and is sacred to the A<u>n</u>angu people of Central Australia. In A<u>n</u>angu culture, Uluṟu marks the site of significant events from the Dreaming, when Creator beings formed the landscape, and it is also the home of their ancestors. On 15 December 1993, Uluṟu became the first icon in Australia to be given back its Aboriginal name. This brought on a wave of dual-named sites and landmarks across the country.

## Wave Rock

Found in inland Western Australia, Wave Rock is known as Katter Kich by the Noongar people. It took 2700 million years to form and is about 15 m tall and 110 m long.

KATTER KICH, WA

**DID YOU KNOW?**

**There are multiple Dreaming stories about Uluṟu that account for the shape and markings on the rock. One tale tells of Tatji – a red lizard who, while out hunting around Uluru, threw his kali (a curved throwing stick), which got it stuck in the rock. As he tried to scoop it out, he left a series of hollows behind.**

# Soil formation

SOIL

Soil starts its life in the form of rocks that are gradually broken down by the process of weathering. Changes in temperature, erosion, weather events and human activity all play a role in weathering rocks. Over hundreds of years, big rocks become little rocks, which are picked up by wind and water and rubbed against each other. Little rocks then become smaller particles and, depending on their size, combine to form different types of soil. It takes hundreds of years to make just a few centimetres of soil!

PLOUGHING SOIL

## What kind of soil?

Weathered particles combine to create many different types of soil. Some rocks are broken down into particles so small that you would need a microscope to view one. These are known as clay particles, while gravel sits at the other end of the size spectrum. Other types of particles include silt and sand. Soil type depends on how much of each particle is included. For example, sticky soils are made mostly of clay, whereas grittier, drier soils have a high sand content. Parent rocks play a big role in the type of soil that is created in certain areas, even having an effect on soil colour. The red soil that is found in many parts of Australia comes from parent rocks that contained a lot of iron.

## Human impact

Soil erosion is a natural process that occurs when wind and rain carry soil away from its original location, which then plays a role in the formation of mountains, valleys and rivers. Human activity has often significantly sped up this process, which can have a negative impact on the environment. First Nations Australians adapted to the environment around them and did little to disturb the soil. The arrival of Europeans in Australia, however, meant the introduction of new animals, crops, and farming techniques that were suited to a different climate. Large areas of land were cleared and used for grazing or ploughed for planting crops. Soil erosion began to occur at a much faster rate.

**DID YOU KNOW?**

**Australia's First Nations peoples are the world's original sustainable farmers, using the soil to grow crops of fruits and grains and harvesting bush tucker as needed.**

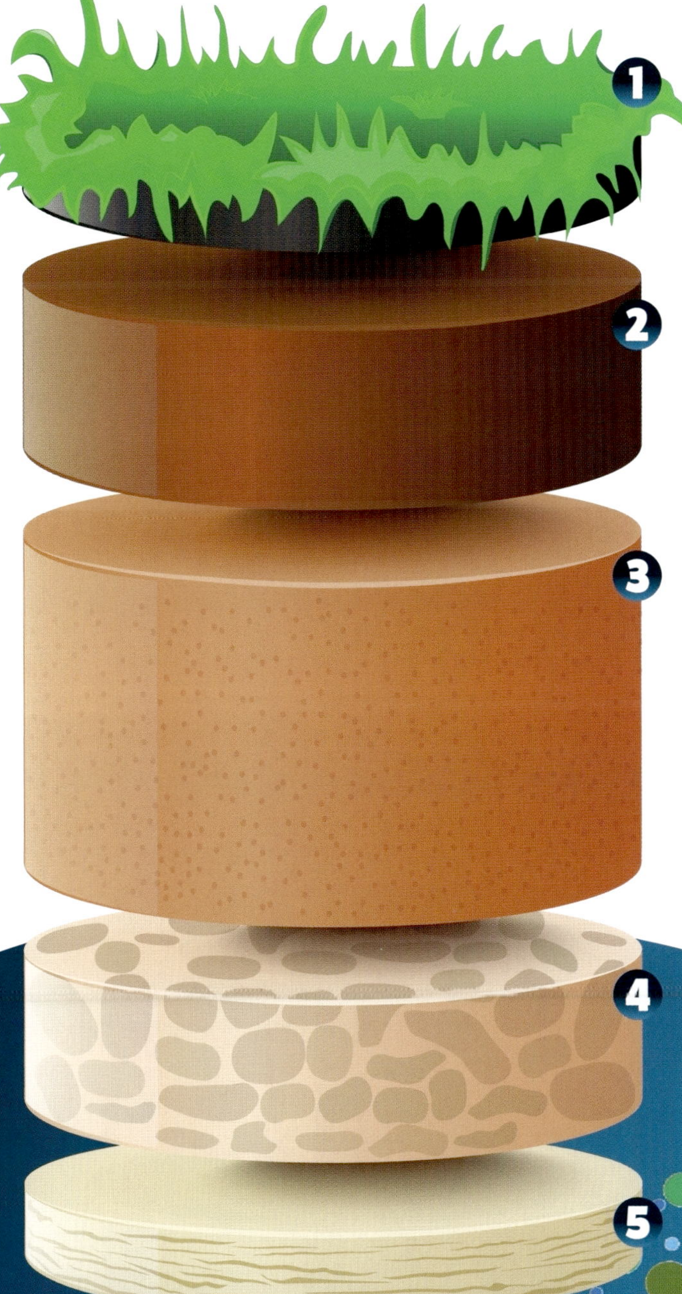


## Soil layers

When we look at soil on the ground, we are only seeing the top layer. Digging deeper reveals the results of hundreds of years of weathering that have occurred, which is displayed in distinct layers known as soil horizons. Looking at all the horizons at once shows us something called a soil profile. Each soil profile is usually made up of three horizons, but may have more.

### 1 Organic layer

The top layer of the horizon is made up of mostly organic material such as leaf litter, and it can be thick or thin.

### 2 Surface horizon

This horizon forms at the surface and is referred to as topsoil. It is made slowly and contains most of the plant food and water. Natural events such as flooding, landslides and volcanic eruptions can sometimes bury the topsoil, which results in it being no longer found at the surface.

**FACT**

A teaspoon of healthy soil contains one billion bacteria, which supports various ecosystems.

### 3 Subsoil horizon

Known as the subsoil, this layer is usually finer than the topsoil and can be found many metres below the surface. It often contains materials such as clay and iron, and holds little food or water. If it is visible, we can tell that some sort of erosion has taken place.

### 4 Substratum horizon

This base horizon is made of parent material, from which the upper horizons were formed. Parent material tells us a lot about what the landscape would have looked like a long time ago, before the weathering process took place and layers were added.

### 5 Bedrock

This is the hard layer at the base of the horizons. It is a mass of solid rock such as basalt, granite, limestone, sandstone or quartzite.

# Volcanoes

In some parts of the world, hot magma forces itself violently up through the Earth's crust and forms areas known as hotspots. As a tectonic plate moves slowly over a hotspot, a volcano can form above that location. Over millions of years, while the plate keeps slowly moving, a chain of volcanoes can form over the same hotspot. Earth's tectonic plates are moving at a speed of up to 10 cm every year, so there are multiple places around the world where these volcanic chains have formed.

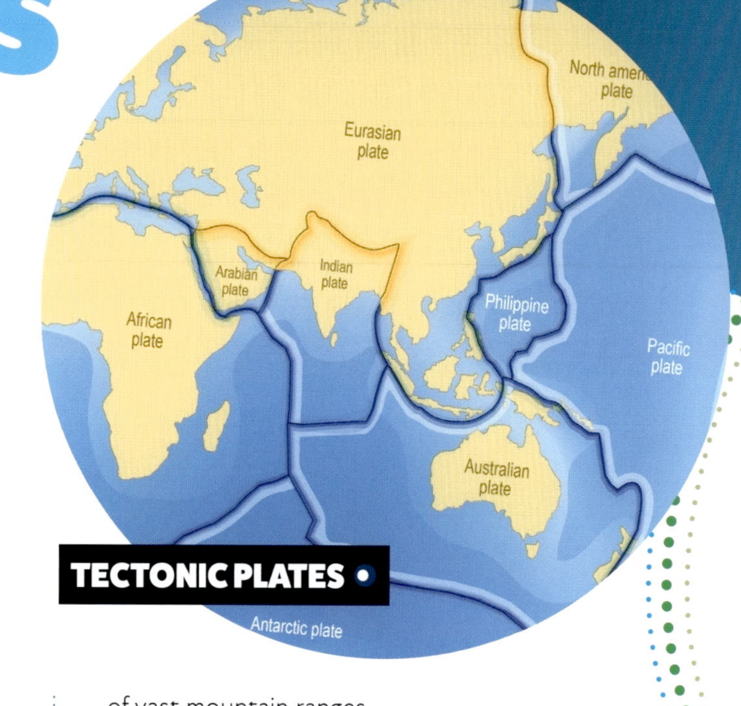


TECTONIC PLATES

## Hotspots

Some hotspots beneath the ocean create volcanoes. These form and then slowly die over many millions of years as the moving plate carries them away. At first, the erupting magma forms an underwater volcano. The mountain grows until it emerges above the ocean surface as a volcanic island.

## Danger zone

Also called the Circum-Pacific Belt, the Ring of Fire is the name given to the belt of weakness in the Earth's crust that extends for 40,000 km from South America to the Alaskan peninsula, Japan, the Philippines, Indonesia and on through the Melanesian islands to New Zealand. The Ring is made up of vast mountain ranges, 452 volcanoes, and deep ocean trenches. Today, the whole area is characterised by frequent earthquakes. The Ring follows the perimeter of the Pacific Plate, which is the tectonic plate that sits below the Pacific Ocean. Dramatic geological events occur when this plate grinds against other plates.

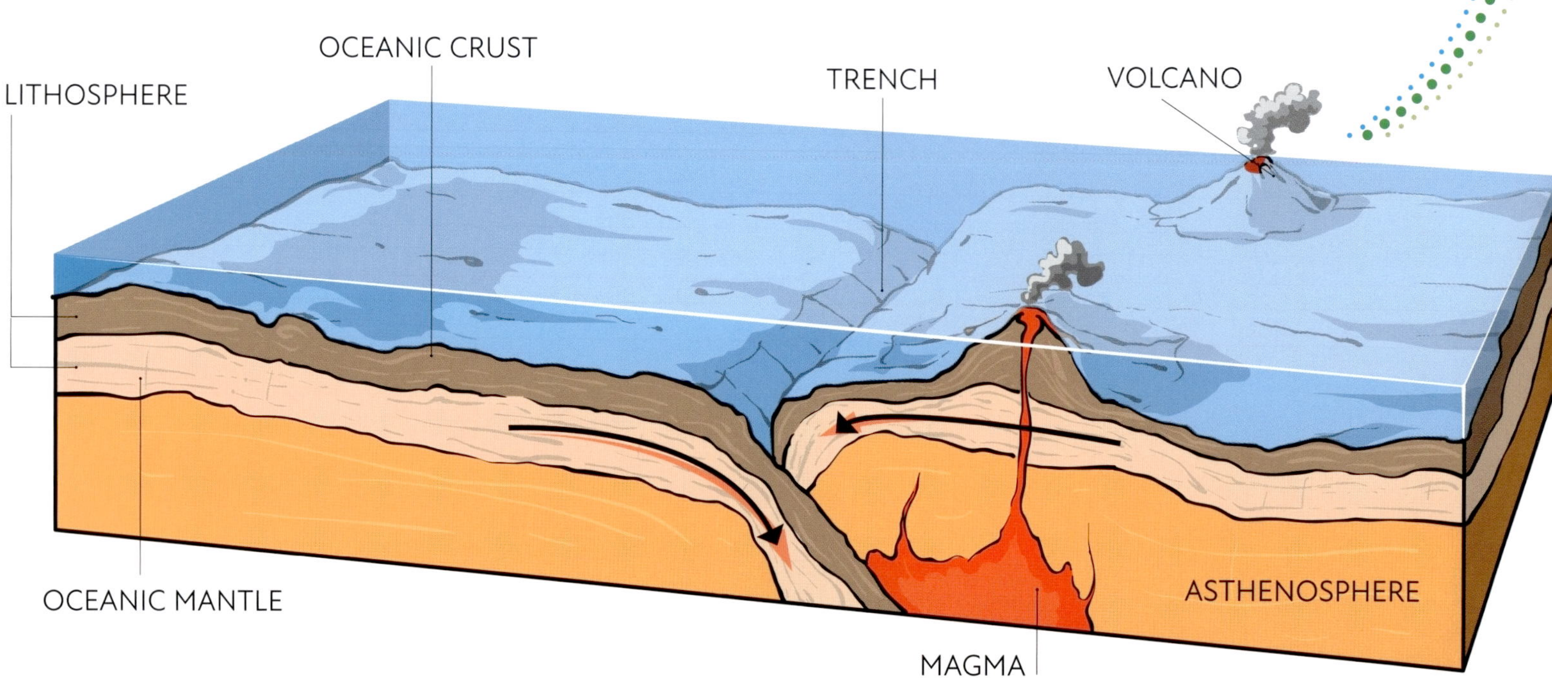

ANAK KRAKATAU, INDONESIA

**FACT**

As long as a hotspot keeps feeding magma into its chambers, a volcano can erupt for many years.

KANDIWAL COUNTRY, WA

## Bigger than a bomb

The largest eruption on human record happened in Indonesia, in 1815 at Mt Tambora. The eruption was 16 times more powerful than the biggest bomb that has ever been detonated. The eruption was responsible for the death of 70,000 people, and it also altered the climate around the world. The temperature dropped, and 1816 came to be known as the 'year without a summer'. The result of this drop in temperature on crops and livestock was enormous, resulting in the worst famine of the 19th century.

HAWAII, USA

## Deadly blasts

In 1883, in west Indonesia on Krakatoa Island, an eruption occurred that is considered one of the deadliest in human history – it is estimated that more than 36,000 people died. At least 70% of the island disappeared, although new island volcanoes appeared over the old caldera in the late 1920s, including Anak Krakatau, which continues to grow today.

## Watch out

This photo (left) of hotspot islands in Hawaii, USA, was taken from space. The largest island is directly over an oceanic hotspot and is made up of five volcanoes. When the other islands were over the spot, each one of them was a volcano too. Now they are slowly sinking back into the sea.

## DID YOU KNOW?

**Scientists believe that an ancient story by Victoria's Gunditjmara people about a volcanic eruption at Budj Bim ( Mt Eccles) is based on true events from 37,000 years ago.**

# Droughts

**Weather patterns play an important role in shaping the Earth's surface and have the power to cause significant and long-term change.**

## Drought impacts

Periods of drought, which often last for months and sometimes even years, can lead to erosion of the land, failure of crops, and animal deaths. It's difficult to define drought, since it is not simply a matter of low rainfall. If that were the case, most of inland Australia would always be in drought. Scientists monitor a number of factors alongside rainfall, such as soil moisture, ground water levels and social expectations, to decide whether an area is in drought or not. Over-consumption by animals, poor farming management, and tree clearing have made the situation worse. Records show that, on average, a severe drought has occurred in Australia once every 18 years.

**Research suggests that the interval between two styles of rock art in the Kimberley could be explained by a severe 1500-year-long drought.**

CRACKED RIVERBED, SA

## How does drought affect the environment?

Every aspect of the land and the creatures it supports is dramatically impacted.

### Habitat destruction

Droughts can cause a widespread loss of vegetation and are especially problematic in agricultural areas where regular irrigation is essential. A prolonged drought might even lead to food shortages.

### Species impact

Animals rely on water as much as humans do, and drought can see many animals, both wild and farmed, die or become sick because of thirst or starvation.

### Desert creation

Drought can lead to greater erosion than usual because of vegetation loss. There's also the issue of the hardening soil and the potential for desertification.

### Water pollution

As dams and watercourses dry up, water quality can decline, which can lead to outbreaks of toxic algae.

### Disaster magnet

Drought increases both the likelihood and severity of bushfires and dust storms.

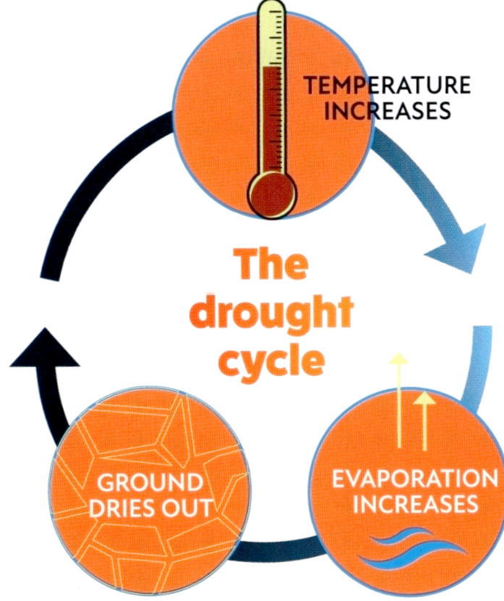


### Rock hard

Drought has several effects on the surface of our Earth. Without rain, rivers and lakes can dry up and sometimes disappear completely. Even soil deep below the surface can dry out. After no rainfall for years at a time, soil becomes rock-hard, and the surface cracks. When rainfall finally arrives after years of drought conditions, the surface is too hard to absorb the water. The result is sudden flash flooding. The runoff collects in valleys and riverbeds, and as more rain falls, the water can often overflow riverbanks and become a fast-flowing flood of water and debris. This is another example of how one instance of extreme weather can lead to more extreme weather events, such as an earthquake causing a tsunami. In this instance, however, the impact of the weather can be felt over many years.

NEPEAN RIVER, NSW

# Floods

As climate change takes hold, floods may happen more frequently. They occur when torrential downpours cannot be absorbed by the soil. When rivers or levees get too full, they burst their banks, spilling water over the land. On the coasts, winds can also whip up huge waves or king tides can flood beaches and estuaries, affecting coastal ecosystems.

## Local trouble

Aside from icy Antarctica, Australia is the driest continent on Earth. However, floods happen frequently here, with a major flood being recorded in all Australian states over the past 150 years. Floods destroy agriculture, infrastructure and homes, and can be fatal, but they're also important to cyclically distribute seeds, animals and sediments to new areas. In northern Australia and parts of the inland, flooding is a seasonal occurrence. During the northern wet season, from November to April, storms replenish the rivers and floodplains.

## The impacts

People have time to move to higher ground or protect their homes with barriers when floodwaters rise slowly. However, the impact is greater when water rises too quickly, as the people affected can get caught in the floods. Buildings and homes are damaged, and vehicles can be washed away. Some people can even drown. It also has widespread effects on the natural environment.

## Plants

Though some native species are more tolerant of waterlogged conditions, for many plants during floods, oxygen is prevented from reaching their roots, which can result in death. Damage to roots is also caused by exposure to the air when surrounding soil is washed away. Even after floodwaters recede, many plants are left vulnerable and likely to be uprooted in windy weather.

## Animals

Many people and animals have died or been injured in flash flooding in Australia. But flooding can also deposit fertile soil on river flats and provide an environment that allows fish, birds and other animals to breed and grow their populations. Floods also trigger other natural events, such as migration and dispersal.

## Rivers

When the Murray River floods, it transforms into a verdant expanse of swamps and waterholes that ripple with life.

## Places

Areas that have already been modified by human activity are more likely to experience greater levels of soil erosion. Removal of vegetation around rivers, dams and coastlines can destabilise existing soil, which is then easily removed by floodwaters.

## Pollutants

While the cycling of sediments and nutrients is essential to a healthy system, too much sediment and nutrients entering a waterway has negative impacts on downstream water quality. Chemicals and hazardous substances can also enter flooding water and contaminate the water bodies it ends up in. In 2011, a tsunami in Japan caused a flood that triggered leakage in nuclear plants and has since led to high radiation in the area.

**DID YOU KNOW?**

**Aboriginal people warned the early settlers not to build towns on the floodplains.**

FLOODWATERS NEAR GYMPIE, QLD

# Fires

Bushfires may be ignited by people accidentally, by lightning, or by incidental friction during extremely dry and hot conditions. Sometimes, people light fires deliberately. The Climate Institute of Australia undertook research and found that extreme fire weather has increased, and the fire season has lengthened across large parts of Australia since the 1970s. If fires are not controlled quickly by trained firefighters, they can develop into raging infernos.

## Part and parcel

Bushfires are part of the Australian landscape. They have been occurring for an estimated 60 million years, and they are a regular cycle in our climate. The most devastating fires are usually preceded by high temperatures, low relative humidity and strong winds, which create ideal conditions for the rapid spread of fire. Australia is the driest inhabited continent, and many areas are covered in eucalypt forests, which burn easily. Fires can spread quickly, especially in summer, when wind sweeps through. Annual bushfires can sometimes escalate to become very dangerous. South-eastern Australia often experiences particularly severe blazes. Although these blazes often destroy homes, claim lives and damage the environment, many native plants have developed characteristics that promote the spread of fire, since it can be necessary for the regeneration of the land and vegetation.

BLUE MOUNTAINS, NSW

## BUSHFIRE SURVIVAL

**For millennia, Aboriginal people managed bushfire-prone land with fire-stick farming techniques such as regular, controlled, cool burns – regimes that land managers have since returned to.**

FIGHTING FIRE

THE AFTERMATH OF A BUSHFIRE

## The impacts

Fires and its smoke affect every aspect of Australia's natural environment.

### Plants

Some plants flower abundantly after a fire, and some take more than a decade to recover. Some desert species burst from seed pods underground, stimulated into growth by heat or smoke. A lack of fire can result in something that is called senescence, which means that these species grow old and die before they have the opportunity to be germinated by fire. In other areas, such as heaths and forests, plants can be killed easily by fire and can be driven out of areas if they face repeated burning.

### Nutrients

High-intensity fires can kill off soil microbes and plant roots, and they can increase the level of nitrogen present in the soil. Fires also alter the nutrient and water levels of the soil, making it more susceptible to runoff and soil erosion.

### Animals

In most environments, animals will recolonise a burnt area after a fire, though this is only possible if the population is high enough – species listed as vulnerable or endangered may not be capable. Insects, reptiles and small mammals will attempt to hide underground; birds are able to fly away (though chicks and eggs are not), and some other arboreal animals may climb into the treetops to escape the flames.

### Pollutants

Toxins, debris and ash released by the fire can run into waterways when rain finally comes, or as the water used to extinguish the fire moves into the waterways. These contaminants can poison sthe water.

### Airways

Fires produce smoke, the inhalation of which can be very dangerous for the elderly, young, infirm or people in enclosed spaces. Fires can also release other chemicals into the air, depending on the environment in which they take place. In built-up areas, where fires damage homes, toxins including mercury, lead and other organic compounds can be released into the air. Fire also releases carbon dioxide into the atmosphere, which contributes to the greenhouse effect.

# Tsunamis

Enormous waves generated by displacement of water in oceans or lakes are called tsunamis. They're most commonly created when tectonic plates move under the ocean floor during an earthquake. But they can also be caused by volcanic eruptions, glacial carving, meteorite impacts or landslides. Every tsunami is different, and not all earthquakes produce them, so it is very difficult to predict where the worst waves will strike and how big they will be.

## How they happen

An earthquake under the ocean jolts the seabed upward. An enormous amount of water is displaced and begins to move outward from the epicentre.

1. Out at sea, the tsunami builds up, and water travels fast – at about the speed of a jet.

2. Coastal water, located in bays and beaches, disappears as it is sucked out into the tsunami.

3. As the tsunami hits the shore, the top of the wave can reach a height of 30 m.

## The impacts

Pushing large volumes of saltwater onto the land, a tsunami affects every part of the environment.

## Animals

Key wildlife habitats can be destroyed in a tsunami. Land animals face the threat of drowning, and sea animals can be killed by polluted waters or the high volume of debris that enters the water.

## Yields

Salination and debris can affect the fertility of soil, which can impact agricultural land and how much produce it is able to yield.

BANTEN PROVINCE, INDONESIA, 2018

## Humans

Tsunamis can have an enormous human impact – not only the loss of life, but also the destruction of housing, infrastructure and agricultural land. Rebuilding after a tsunami, like many extreme weather events, can take a very long time.

## Plants

Trees and plants can be uprooted in a tsunami, leaving whole stretches of land empty. Areas such as wetlands, coral reefs, mangroves and beaches are naturally more susceptible. Plant loss can cause higher levels of erosion and changes in the landscape long after the tsunami has occurred.

## Pollutants

Freshwater bodies such as rivers, wells and lakes can become briny and undrinkable without purification, affecting people, plants and animals.There is also the chance that toxic chemicals will be displaced during a tsunami and pollute the waterways that they eventually run into.

**DID YOU KNOW?**

**More than 50 tsunamis have been recorded across Australia, with one of the largest hitting WA's Cape Leveque in 1977. The waves were 6 m in height.**

*A coral reef destroyed by a tsunami.*

# Deforestation

The razing and felling of forests expels billions of tonnes of carbon dioxide into the atmosphere each year. That's roughly as much as the entire global transport sector, including every single petrol-burning car, truck, boat, train and aeroplane on Earth. That's scary if you're a resident orangutan or a tree kangaroo, but it should concern humans too. The rampant clearing of forests imperils us all, even if we live too far away to hear the growl of the approaching bulldozers.

## Green matters

Rainforests sustain an astonishing diversity of species and keep our planet livable by limiting soil erosion, reducing floods, stabilising the climate and maintaining natural water cycles. When undisturbed, forests store a great deal of carbon, keeping it safely locked up in their biomass rather than in the atmosphere where it accelerates global warming. Yet roughly 10 million hectares of tropical forest are destroyed every year – the equivalent of 30 football fields a minute.

**TAKAYNA / TARKINE, TAS**

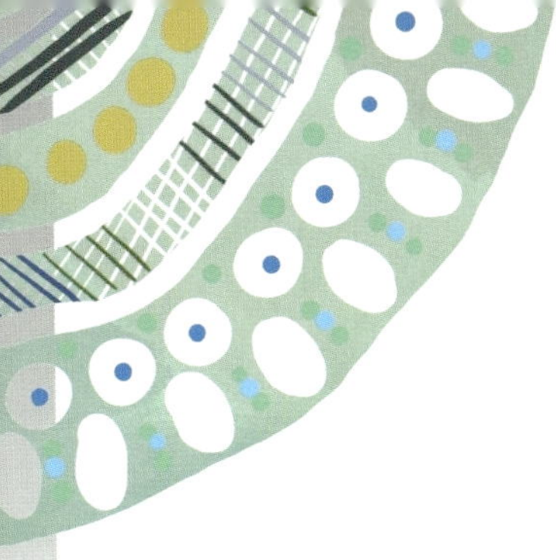

## Planting trees

Australia has been working hard to correct the balance, and the 20 Million Trees Program did just that. More than 29.5 million trees were planted over 30,000 ha. In even better news, New South Wales recently set a zero extinction target for its national parks, to help protect its almost 1000 endangered plants and animals.

## Keeping cool

Tropical forests, which emit water vapour into the atmosphere, are major drivers of cloud formation. Clouds cool the planet by reflecting solar heat back into space, and they also sustain regional rainfall, which limits destructive forest fires. Hence, saving a hectare of tropical forest does far more to reduce global warming than saving a hectare of other types of forest.

### DID YOU KNOW?

**The Traditional Custodians of the Daintree Rainforest call it Kaba Kada – which appropriately means 'rainy place'.**

*Fruit bats need our forests, and we need them to help pollinate more trees.*

PRECIPITATION

CONDENSATION

EVAPORATION

COLLECTION

## Rainforest life

From their damp forest floors to their dense canopies, tropical rainforests are home to complex ecosystems that support a wide range of wildlife biodiversity. The Daintree Rainforest is home to at least 12,000 different types of insect, 113 species of reptile, and 368 bird species – including the Southern Cassowary, which is Australia's heaviest native bird, weighing up to 76 kg.

# Water works case study:

## Redfern Jarjum College

Sydney's sandstone cliffs and beaches are a great demonstration of how this ancient land has been shaped by relentless tides and winds. Some of the kids from Redfern Jarjum College engaged in activities to demonstrate how water works to shape the Earth's surface.

The Jarjums had a discussion prior to the investigation and decided to link the ideas they came up with to their trip to Little Bay Beach earlier in the year. Under the COVID restrictions in NSW at the time of this investigation, students at the school conducted the demonstrations, while remote learners watched on and contributed their ideas through a video call.

Using trays filled with sand, the Jarjums were able to investigate the effect of waves lapping at the coast and how destructive large tidal surges can be. In the first part of their demonstration, the students observed how regular, small waves gradually formed a beach that served to protect the cliffs as the water ran up the sand, losing its energy.

Weather can have a big impact, with winds causing more frequent and larger waves. Students demonstrated this by moving the wave-machine (container lid) back and forth at a faster rate.

Similarly, tides cause the water level to increase or decrease. This was demonstrated by adding water to their model. With more water, the beaches were overrun, causing the cliffs to crumble and fall into the sea.

Next, the students used a larger tray and a watering can to model the effects of rain on the land. Again, they chatted

## SHAPING THE LAND

**The experiments showed that weather events like heavy rain impact upon Earth's surfaces.**

about what they knew and had seen of the water's impact when it rained. Students talked about it running down slopes and forming into streams and puddles.

On the model landscape, students created some peaks to simulate the higher ground of hills or mountains. The DeadlyScientists observed the way the rain gathered in streams and carved channels into their model landscape, like rivers forming valleys. This left some high peaks on the landscape, just as hills and mountains remained when gullies, canyons and valleys were created over time.

The students then decided to plan a trip up north to the Hawkesbury River area, on Darug Country, where they would be able to see this effect on a grand scale.

# DEADLY SCIENCE

## Earth's changing surfaces

First published in 2021, reprinted in 2023

52–54 Turner Street
Redfern NSW 2016

editorial@ausgeo.com.au
australiangeographic.com.au

**Series Editor:** Corey Tutt
**Illustrations:** Mim Cole / Mimmim

**Commissioning Editor:** Karin Cox
**Chief Sub-Editor:** Serene Conneeley
**Editor:** Michele Perry
**Creative Director:** Aleksandra Beare
**Designer:** Harmony Southern
**Print Production:** Andy Franks

AUSTRALIAN GEOGRAPHIC
Managing Director: David Haslingden
Director of Content: Liz Ginis
Licensing and Publishing Manager: Tom Bates
Commercial Assistant: Felicity McManus

Printed in China by LEO Paper Products LTD.

A catalogue record for this book is available from the National Library of Australia

## Picture credits

**Front Cover:** FotoDuets/Shutterstock (SS); Designua/SS; Mopic/SS; Drew Hopper/Australian Geographic (AG); Darky Doors/SS; Johan Swanepoel/SS; KrimKate/SS. **2:** FoxGrafy/SS. **3:** Olga Sanylenko/SS; SS; Science Photo Library/Alamy. **4:** VectorMine/SS. **5:** Deco/Alamy; Benny Marty/SS; Catmando/SS; VectorMine/SS. **6:** sirtravelalot/SS; Nadezda Murmakova/SS. **7:** VectorMine/SS. **8:** Annette Spinks/SS. **9:** Alex Cimbal/SS; Karin Cox/AG; LittlePanda29/SS; SF Photo/SS; Ale_Koziura/SS. **10:** Robyn Mackenzie/SS; Kasin/SS; AG. **11:** AG. **12:** AG. **13:** Benny Marty/SS; State Government of Victoria/First Peoples - State Relations; vvoe/SS. **14–15:** Maurizio De Mattei/SS. **15:** Travelling.About/SS; PhotopankPL/SS. **16:** lovelyday12/SS; fotookamziky/SS; oticki/SS.**17:** Michael Leslie/SS; Designua/SS. **18:** Designua/SS; EreborMountain/SS. **19:** Philip Schubert/SS; feygraphy/SS/ AG. **20:** Nils Versemann/SS; Robert Mcgillivray/SS. **21:** kwest/SS; FiledIMAGE/SS; roibu/SS. **22:** Annie 888/SS; Phillip Wittke/SS; St Lermy/SS; Shmelly50/SS. **23:** Hypervision Creative/SS. **24:** Leah-Anne Thompson/SS. **25:** Robyn Mackenzie/SS; KARL HOFMAN/SS; carti77/SS; Toa55/SS. **26–27:** Kurniawan Rizqi/SS; AG. **27:** Kurniawan Rizqi/SS; Ethan Daniels/SS. **28:** Tom Jastram/SS; **29:** Greg Brave/SS; EcoPrint/SS; Anna L. e Marina Durante/SS. **30–31:** Deadly Science.

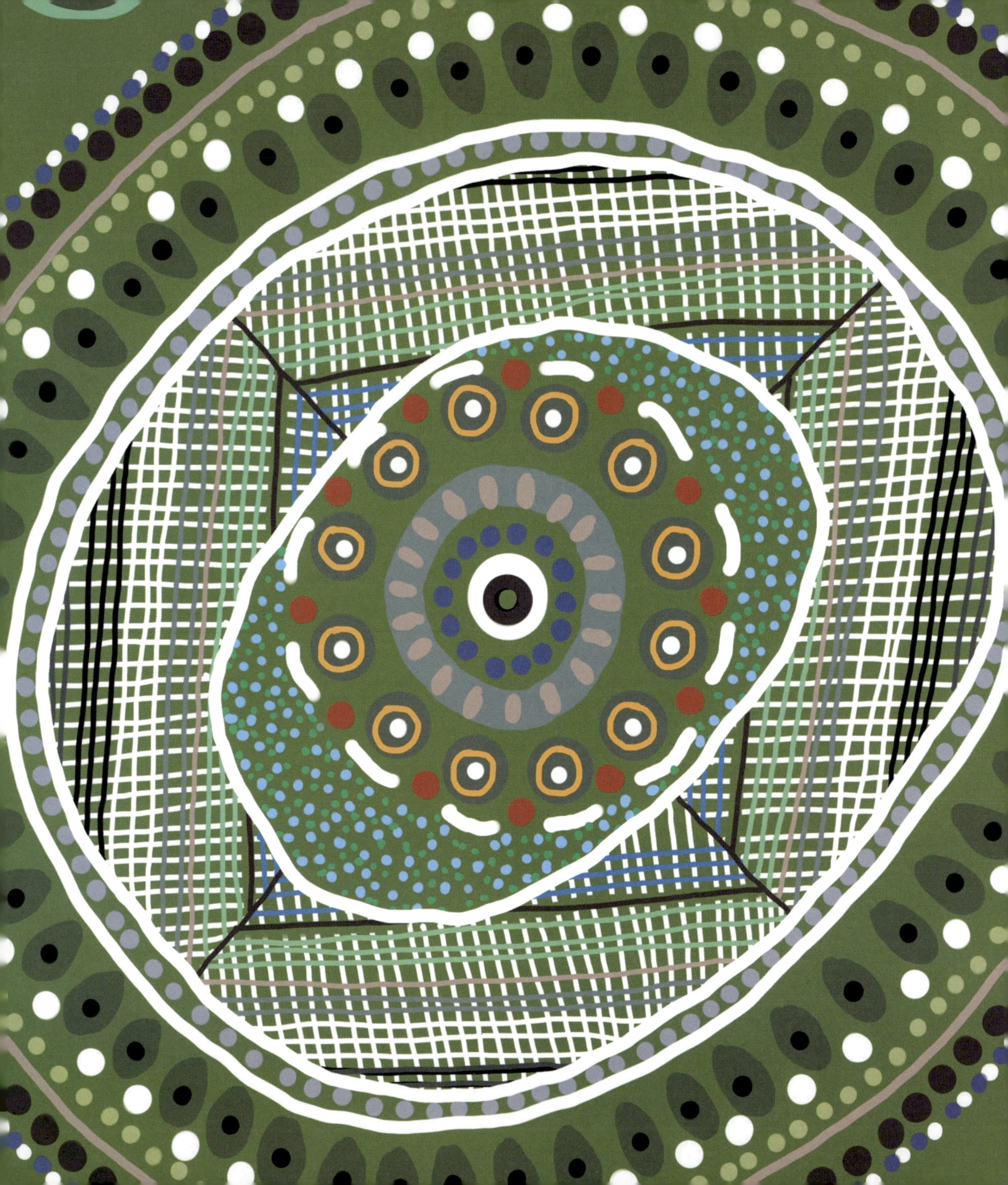